Tedd Arnold

Scholastic Inc.

Photo credits: Front cover: © Stephen Frink/Getty Images (RF); back cover: © Seapics.com: pp. 4–5: © Audubon Nature Institute; p. 6 (top): © iStockphoto; p. 6 (center): © FAUP/Shutterstock; p. 6 (bottom): © Thinkstock (RF); p. 7 (top left): © Ginet -Drin/age fotostock; p. 7 (top right): © Dan Burton/age fotostock; p. 7 (center): © Seapics.com; p. 7 (bottom): © W. Scott/Shutterstock; pp. 8–9: © Seapics.com; p. 9 (top right): © Seapics.com; p. 10 (bottom): © Carlos Villoch/age fotostock; p. 11 (top): © Jim Agronick/Shutterstock; p. 11 (bottom): © Seapics.com; p. 12 (top): © Seapics.com; p. 12 (bottom): © Seapics.com; p. 13 (top): © Andy Murch/Vwpics/Newscom; p. 13 (bottom): © MP cz/Shutterstock; pp. 14–5: © Willyam Bradberry/Shutterstock; p. 16 (top): © iStockphoto; p. 17 (top): © Bill Curtsinger/National Geographic Stock; p. 17 (bottom): © Jurgen Freund/NPL/Minden Pictures; p. 18 (top): © Dray van Beeck/Shutterstock; p. 18 (bottom): © Seapics.com; p. 19 (top): © Thinkstock (RF); p. 19 (center): © Seapics.com; p. 19 (bottom): © Seapics.com; pp. 20–21: © Lawrence Cruciana/Shutterstock; p. 21 (top): © Seapics.com; p. 21 (bottom): © Thinkstock (RF); p. 22 (top): © Seapics.com; p. 22 (bottom): © Seapics.com; p. 23 (center): © Reinhard Dirscherl/age fotostock; p. 24 (top): © Stuart Keasley/age fotostock; pp. 24–25: © Marevision/age fotostock; pp. 26–7: © Thinkstock (RF); p. 28 (top): © David Doubilet/National Geographic Stock; p. 28 (bottom): © Yasumasa Kobayashi/Nature Production/Minden Pictures; p. 29 (top): © Jason Edwards/National Geographic Stock; p. 29 (bottom): © Doug Perrine/Nature Picture Library; p. 30 (top): © Norbert Probst/imageb/age fotostock; p. 30 (bottom): © Seapics.com; p. 31 (bottom): © Bill Curtsinger /National Geographic Stock.

ISBN 978-0-545-50771-4

12 11 10 9 14 15 16 17/0

Printed in the U.S.A. 40
First printing, January 2013

A boy had a pet fly named Fly Guy.
Fly Guy could say the boy's name —

Buzz and Fly Guy were at the aquarium (ah-KWEAR-ee-um).

"Let's go see the sharks!" said Buzz.

Fly Guy seemed scared.

“Sharks are cool!” said Buzz. “There’s nothing to be afraid of here at the aquarium.”

They dived in to find out more....

Scientists have found about 400 different kinds of sharks. Each shark has amazing abilities.

SPINY
DOGFISH SHARK
BASKING SHARK
PREHISTORIC
SHARK
Sharks have
been around
for over 400
million years!
PREHISTORIC
SHARK TOOTH

Sharks are fish. They live in bodies of water all over the world—even in lakes and rivers!

GILLZZ
BULL SHARK

A shark's skeleton is made of cartilage (KAR-tuh-lij). Sharks don't have any bones.

Cartilage makes sharks flexible. They can turn quickly to catch a bite to eat.

Sharks have many rows of teeth. Only the front row is used for eating.

JAWS OF A
SAND TIGER SHARK
SAND TIGER
SHARK

Most sharks are carnivores (KAR-nih-vorz). They eat meat, such as fish and seagulls.

A shark uses its sharp teeth to rip its prey. Then the shark swallows the meat whole—without even chewing!

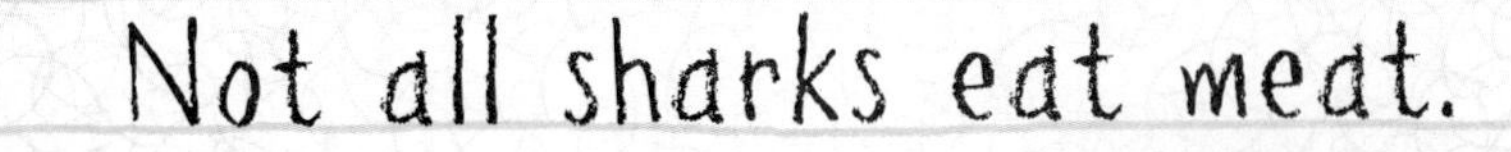

Not all sharks eat meat.

The whale shark is the largest shark in the world. It eats a small plant called plankton and other tiny plants.

Close-up of whale-shark teeth!

Most sharks have rough skin made of denticles (DEN-tih-kuhlz).

BLUE SHARK

It feels hard and sharp. Denticles protect sharks from harm.

A BLUE SHARK'S TINY DENTICLES

GREAT WHITE SHARK

ROUGH AND TOUGH!

A GREAT WHITE SHARK'S DENTICLES

A GREENLAND SHARK'S DENTICLES

NURSE SHARK

Nurse sharks have smoother skin than most sharks. It feels like sandpaper.

Other fish have smooth, slippery scales. A shark's teeth can bite right through them.

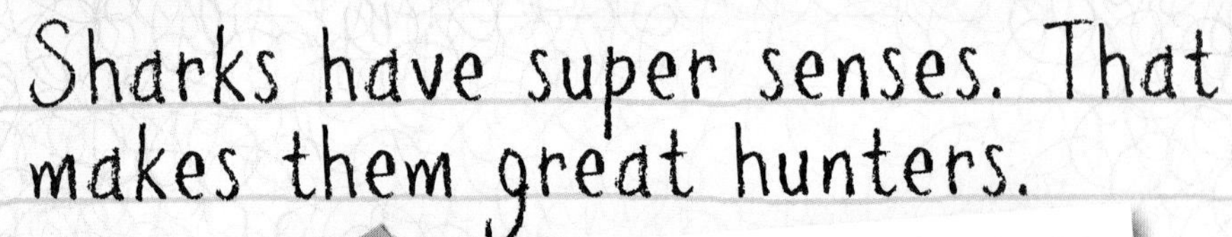

Sharks have super senses. That makes them great hunters.

Moses smoothhound shark

Bigeye houndshark

A shark can hear its prey moving underwater! It can even hear a fish's muscles moving as it swims.

whitetip reef shark

LESSER SPOTTED DOGFISH
(SMALL SPOTTED CATSHARK)

A shark has special eyesight that helps it to navigate (NAV-ih-gayt) through dark, murky water.

People need special glasses to see in the dark.
But a shark can feel its prey nearby without even seeing it!

Sharks are very smart. They have brains—just like humans and flies.

They have supersensitive noses to sniff out their next meal. Two-thirds of a shark's brain is used for smelling.

A great white shark can smell blood from 3 miles away!

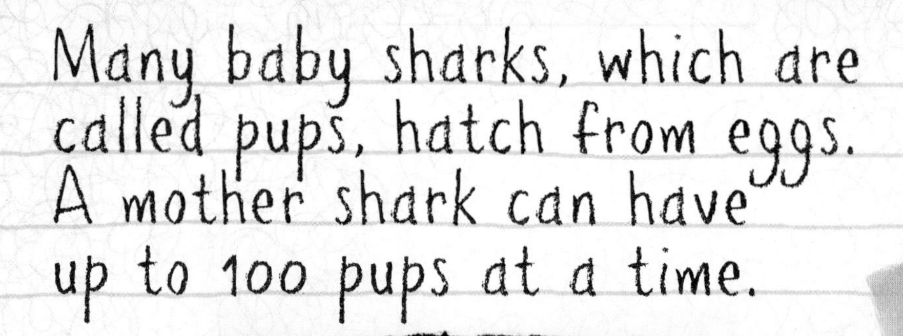

Many baby sharks, which are called pups, hatch from eggs. A mother shark can have up to 100 pups at a time.

A swell shark embryo within the egg.

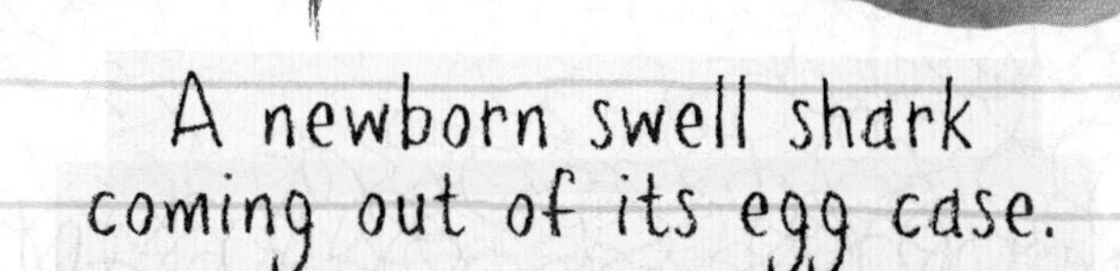

A newborn swell shark coming out of its egg case.

A newborn shark pup resting!

Most sharks live to be about 25 years old. That's way longer than the life of a fly!

A newborn lemon shark pup swimming away from its mother.

Sharks do not sleep. Most have to keep moving in order to breathe!

Sharks are superfast swimmers. They can move at up to 25 miles per hour! But they cannot swim backward.

Some sharks are nocturnal (nok-TUR-nuhl) hunters. They are more active at night.

In the dark, a cookie-cutter shark uses a special light called luminescence (loo-mih-NEH-suhns). This light makes the shark look smaller so that its prey is not scared away. The shark surprises its prey and takes a cookie-sized bite!

"Wow!" said Buzz. "We learned a lot about sharks today. They are so cool!"

Fly Guy was not scared anymore.

"Fly Guy," said Buzz, "I can't wait for our next field trip!"